PETERSEN, Palle
Vikings   J.N.F.

Petersen, Palle
  Vikings.—(Beans).
  1. Vikings
  I. Title
  948'.02   DL65

ISBN 0-7136-2039-0

A & C Black (Publishers) Limited
35 Bedford Row, London WC1R 4JH
© 1980 (English text) A & C Black (Publishers) Limited
© 1978 Palle Petersen
© 1978 (illustrations) Borgens Forlag Copenhagen

Acknowledgments

The publishers are grateful to the following
for permission to reproduce photographs: Michael
Holford Library 17c, Manx Technical Publications
Ltd 27, Ann Münchow 13, York Archaeological
Trust 4, 5.

The English text is by Ruth Marris
The drawings are by Gabrielle Stoddart
The map is by Tony Garrett

Printed in Great Britain by
Hazell Watson & Viney Ltd, Aylesbury, Bucks.

Vikings

Palle Petersen

Adam & Charles Black · London

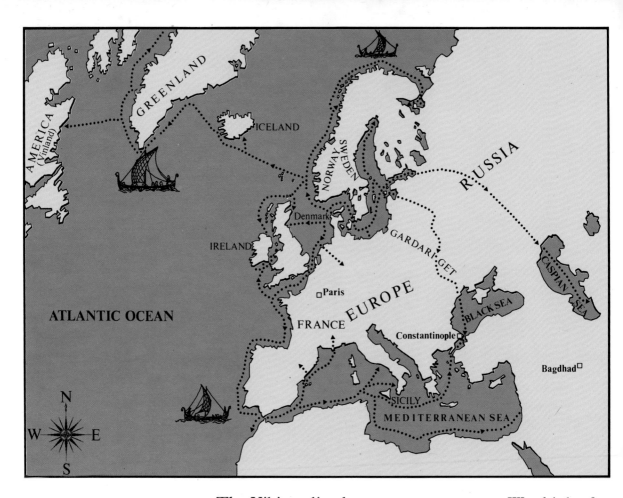

The Vikings lived over 1000 years ago. We think of them now as great sea-voyagers who came from the north to raid and murder. Later they settled in the lands they had first plundered.

Their wanderings took them westwards to North America (Vinland) via Iceland and Greenland, and eastwards to the Mediterranean, Constantinople, Baghdad and Russia.

We know most about the Vikings from writers living in the countries they attacked. Reports of their raids weren't very favourable. The Anglo-Saxon Chronicle records their attack on the monastery of Lindisfarne in AD 783

> In this year . . . the harrying of the heathen miserably destroyed God's church in Lindisfarne . . .

At first, the Vikings had no written history. They told stories that were passed down from one generation to another. We can learn more about them from the Bayeux Tapestry. You can see part of the Tapestry below. It shows the Viking ships that brought the Norman invaders to England in 1066.

Without written history, we have to rely on what archaeologists can tell us. They have uncovered weapons, tools, jewellery, skeletons and the remains of buildings.

In Dublin and York, both important Viking towns, archaeologists have found many things which help us to understand life in Viking times. You can see some of those from York in the colour photographs on these two pages.

The Vikings didn't just appear overnight and start making their journeys. There was a good reason for what they did. There was a shortage of fertile land in the countries they came from, so the young and adventurous went to seek better land elsewhere. Sometimes a ship set off alone; sometimes a small fleet set off.

▲ Two Viking workshops   ▼ A wooden cup and bowls

All the people in the north were closely bound together because they spoke the same language, shared the same history and were of the same religion. The Northmen (the word *Viking* wasn't used until much later) also buried their dead in the same way.

The graves of rich Vikings can tell us a great deal about them. At the top of these two pages you can see a collection of items from a wealthy woman's grave.

There are pins, buckles, brooches and clasps as well as bowls, combs and keys. The keys were for opening chests of clothes and valuables. Many keys meant many chests and therefore great wealth.

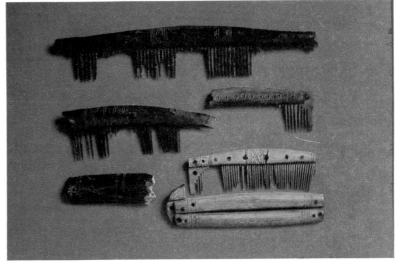

▲ Antler combs

▼ A boot on a bone ice-skate

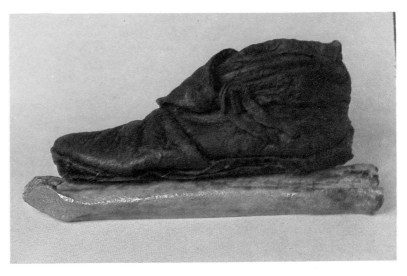

The row of skulls in the top picture was uncovered in Greenland. Archaeologists can find traces of diseases these people suffered from by examining their skeletons. Many of them had gout. One of them was probably killed in a fight as a knife was found sticking between his ribs.

In the bottom picture you can see another archaeologist examining a skull. This skull came from a grave that contained a strip of rusty metal, which turned out to be a sword. A bronze boss was all that remained of a shield.

The dead Viking's horse was buried with its owner, and parts of its skeleton were also found.

In the picture below you can see a man dressed up to look like the Viking whose grave the archaeologist has studied. He would have been about the same height as an average man today. We can tell from his bones that he was about forty years old when he died.

The man in the picture carries copies of the sword and the shield found in the grave. Most Vikings were buried with their riding equipment, their weapons, and often their horses as well.

A modern man dressed up to look like a Viking

In the thirteenth century Viking stories began to be written down. Two famous writers were Snorri Sturluson, who wrote about events in Iceland, and Saxo Grammaticus, who wrote a history of Denmark. These stories are known as sagas.

Storytellers (scalds) were respected and well-paid men. They sang and composed ballads about kings' and warriors' successes in battle, as well as reciting whole sagas. They travelled from place to place and entertained Vikings as they sat around the fireside in the chieftan's hall.

The Vikings had many gods. They sacrificed people and animals to the gods, like the horse in this picture. They told a story of how the world began and how their gods were born.

At first there was nothing, only a great void called Ginnungagap. To the north was a dark, cold place with freezing rivers called Niflheim. To the south was Muspell, fiery and hot.

Where the two places met, fog was created. The fog turned into raindrops. Two of the drops became a giant called Ymir and a cow who fed him called Audumbla.

Ymir created the parents of the gods, who in turn gave birth to the first gods—Odin, Vili, and Ve. The gods lived in a place called Asgard.

Odin, Vili and Ve killed Ymir. They turned his body into the earth (Midgard), his blood into the seas and his bones into the mountains.

Odin was the greatest of the gods. He found two trees on the seashore and from them made the first man and the first woman in Midgard. He lived in Valhalla, in Asgard, and controlled all the battles in the world. The Vikings preferred to die in battle so that they could go to Valhalla and join Odin.

Another god was Thor. He was strong and always fighting the giants, who were the gods' enemies. He made thunder and lightning with his hammer. Many Vikings wore a miniature Thor's hammer round their necks, like the crosses some Christians wear.

▲ Thor, holding his hammer, tries to capture the Midgard serpent which is wrapped around the earth

A miniature Thor's hammer

Odin riding his eight-legged horse Slepnir

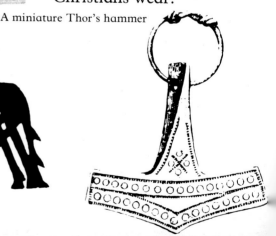

The Scandinavian countries kept their own religion. The rest of Europe became Christian.

Charlemagne, Christian king of the Franks, wanted to invade Denmark. He was prevented by Godfred, the Danish king, who had a large fleet and had built a fortification called the *Danevirke* to keep the Franks out.

Because history was written down by Christian monks at this time, Charlemagne's attack on Denmark was highly praised. But the Vikings didn't get praised by Christian historians. People used to say this Latin prayer.

A furore Normanorum, libera nos domine

From the fury of the Northmen, Lord deliver us.

▲ Charlemagne, king of the Franks

▼ Vikings attacking a monastery.

The Vikings' most powerful weapon was their ships. In nearly all other European countries the sea was feared. Few vessels ventured out of sight of land. They always sailed alongside the shore.

The Vikings built wide flat-bottomed ships on a low keel. Ships designed like the one in the picture below could carry a large sail, travel quickly and sail right up to a beach. This ship has been preserved in Norway.

On this page we can see the ship as the archaeologists first found it. It was in a burial mound. Kings and queens were often buried in a ship with their gold and silver valuables.

An Anglo-Saxon king in England was buried like this, in a ship, at Sutton Hoo in Suffolk. All the treasure from the Norwegian ship was stolen by robbers a thousand years ago, but the treasure from Sutton Hoo can still be seen in the British Museum in London.

Five Viking ships were found underwater in the Roskilde fjord in Denmark. They were sunk on purpose to block the channel to the town of Roskilde and protect it from attack.

The ships were found in thousands of pieces, as the top picture shows.

In the bottom picture you can see one of the ships being put together in a museum.

The five ships show the different types of vessels the Vikings used. There were two warships, two traders and one ferry.

Warships, or longships, sailed the fastest but they were very heavy to row. In battle, dragon heads were attached to their prows to frighten the enemy. You can see a picture of one below. The heads were taken off in harbour because they were thought to bring bad luck.

A modern replica of a Viking ship ▶
sailing today

▼ The prow of a Viking ship

▼ A ship-building scene from the Bayeux Tapestry

The Vikings got bolder as their ships became faster.
They attacked London, and even sailed up the river
Seine to Paris.

The Swedish Vikings took over some land in
Russia and called it Gardariget. All the
Vikings wanted land and trade. It was
much better than raiding.

A Viking expedition looked a bit like a
camping trip. They took tents, pots,
plates and buckets. Barrels held
salted meat, and wine and water
were carried in leather bags.
They sailed by the stars or
the sun because the compass
had not yet been invented.

Once the Vikings had land, they began to develop trade. The Vikings sold skins, cattle, grain, fish, cloth and slaves. They bought clothes, silk, glass, wine, and most important of all, metal. From the metal they made their weapons.

Market towns grew up, and merchants and craft workers lived and traded in them. In the photograph above, you can see what the house of a wealthy merchant might have looked like. The house was built by archaeologists. The cart and boat are copies of vehicles the merchant might have owned.

Christianity gradually reached the north. Many Vikings were converted because Christian merchants would only trade with other Christians.

The Vikings found Christianity hard to understand. The fact that Jesus had been crucified like a common criminal didn't appeal to them. Some priests bribed Vikings with christening presents. One Viking was baptised twenty times, and so got twenty presents.

The large decorated stone in the photograph opposite tells the story of the conversion of King Harald Bluetooth of Denmark. On one side is a carving of Christ crucified. On another is a large ox fighting with a snake. This may symbolise the Christians' victory over the Vikings.

The third side of the stone has an inscription on it which claims that Harald converted all the Danes. This wasn't really true. It took much longer for Christianity to reach remote areas. The inscription says

Harald the king set up this stone to his father Gorm and his mother Tyra. Harald who won all Denmark and Norway and made the Danes Christian.

ᚼᛅᚱᛅᛚᛏᚱ:ᚴᚢᚾᚢᚴᛦ:ᛒᛅᚦ:ᚴᛅᚢᚱᚢᛅ
haraltr kunukʀ þaþ kaurua

ᚴᚢᛒᛚ:ᚦᛅᚢᛋᛁ:ᛅᚠᛏ:ᚴᚢᚱᛘᚠᛅᚦᚢᚱ ᛋᛁᚾ
kubl þausi aft kurmfaþur sin

ᛅᚢᚴ ᛅᚠᛏ:ᚦᛅᚢᚱᚢᛁ:ᛘᚢᚦᚢᚱ:ᛋᛁᚾᛅ:ᛋᛅ
auk aft þąurui muþur sina sa

ᚼᛅᚱᛅᛚᛏᚱ:ᛁᛅᛋ:ᛋᛅᛦ.ᚢᛅᚾ.ᛏᛅᚾᛘᛅᚢᚱᚴ
haraltr ias sąʀ uan tanmaurk

ᛅᛚᛅ.ᛅᚢᚴ.ᚾᚢᚱᚢᛁᛅᚴ.ᛅᚢᚴ.ᛏᛅᚾᛁ.ᚴᛅᚱᚦᛁ.ᚴᚱᛁᛋᛏᚾᛅ
ala auk nuruiak auk tani karþi kristną

The kings of Norway, Sweden and Denmark were always attacking each other. Harald Bluetooth conquered Norway as well as Denmark. His son Svein Forkbeard seized power in Denmark by allowing his father to be killed. Svein was responsible for building camps for training Viking warriors. You can see a model of one of his camps below.

Meanwhile, in Norway, Olav Trygvasson became king. He forced all the Norwegians to become Christians. People weren't very eager to be converted. Svein, with help from Sweden, decided this was a good time to attack Norway. He defeated Olav's fleet, Olav died in the battle, and Svein became king of Norway as well as Denmark.

Svein was now in control of the Danish, Norwegian and Swedish fleets, and so he was strong enough to conquer a large part of England. His son, Knud the Great (Canute) later became king of England and married the English queen.

While Knud was in England, Olav the Stout became king of Norway. He too forced Christianity on the Norwegians, and again they rebelled. In the end they defeated and killed Olav. Olav was later made a saint when the Norwegians finally became Christians.

Olav the Stout fighting the Norwegian farmers

We usually hear most about the famous people in history. But they couldn't have been famous without a lot of help.

It was the younger sons of farmers, who wouldn't inherit land, who rowed the Viking ships that carried kings to their conquests. They were the ones who finally settled in Normandy, England, Ireland, Sicily and Russia, for there they found the land they wanted.

Farmers used slaves for heavy work. Slaves are not always remembered in history, but they were important. Without them, the Vikings wouldn't have had time to go voyaging.

At first kings were elected, but in time royal power was inherited. The kings installed earls throughout their countries to collect taxes and to keep peace. The money was used for armies and ships.

Knud the Great is a good example of a Viking king. He ruled Denmark, Norway and England. Although he was a Christian, he ruled harshly and killed anyone who opposed him.

But Knud died and his empire fell apart. Later, Harald Hardrada of Norway tried to reunite it. But he was killed and defeated by King Harold Godwinson of England at the battle of Stamford Bridge in 1066.

Harold wasn't successful for long. A few weeks later he was defeated at the battle of Hastings by William of Normandy, descendant of a Viking. In the picture we can see King Harold embroidered on the Bayeux Tapestry.

Iceland was the place where Viking history was first recorded by the Vikings themselves. The Icelandic sagas read like exciting novels.

One of them tells how the Norwegians first settled in Iceland. It's called *Eric the Red's Saga*. Eric had caused trouble in Norway and was forced to leave. He sailed west to Iceland followed by other families bringing slaves and animals. The Icelandic settlement flourished and founded the world's first parliament, the *Alting*, which was held at Tingvellir.

But although the Alting was the first parliament, the oldest continuous parliament belongs to the Isle of Man, where it has met for over 1000 years. It too was founded by the Vikings and, every midsummer day, laws are still made on Tynwald Hill. You can see a picture of the hill below.

An aerial view of Tynwald Hill

Eric the Red also got into trouble in Iceland. He killed some men and was outlawed by the Alting. So he sailed west again and founded a settlement in Greenland. It was more snowy than green, but he thought the name would attract settlers.

Many farmers left Iceland to join Eric the Red's settlement. But when they got there they discovered a very hard life: the winters were long and cold; there wasn't enough food, nor enough sun to ripen crops; and weapons and equipment had to be brought by ship from Norway. The sea was often frozen and the ships couldn't get through.

◄ An archaeologist excavating Eric the Red's farm

On a journey back from Norway, Eric's son Leif was blown off course in a storm. Leif discovered a new land which he named Vinland (grass-land). This was North America.

Next year an expedition set off for Vinland, but the ships never got there. A third trip was made the following year. In Vinland the Vikings encountered American Indians whom they called *Skraelings*.

At first the Skraelings and Vikings traded peacefully together, but trouble soon developed. Eric's son Thorstein was killed, and the settlement eventually had to move back to Greenland, where it lasted until about AD 1400. Cold, starvation and possibly Eskimo attacks gradually killed off the remaining Vikings.

The age of the Vikings came to an end in the twelfth century. By then the Viking north had become just another part of Christian Europe.

Christian churches were built throughout Viking territory. This fine wooden church is in Norway. Many of the carvings will remind you of the Viking past. There are dragon heads on the gables like the ones on Viking ships.

But although the Vikings were now Christians, they still fought over trade.

These days we have disagreements about the same sorts of things. Although we don't raid and plunder like the Vikings did, we can often get goods very cheaply from poorer countries. When these goods become very important to us, we use force to protect our trade.

Although we don't have slaves to work for us like the Vikings did, there are still a lot of poor people working for a few rich people. In many ways things have changed greatly since the time of the Vikings—but in some ways things are still very much the same.

A crucifix from a Danish church, dating from about AD 1050